Eco Journeys

LIFE OF A PIECE OF PAPER

by Louise Nelson

Minneapolis, Minnesota

Credits

Front cover - Diego Cervo, Robert Neumann, WhiteYura. 3 - Roman Samokhin/Shutterstock. 4&5 - Friends Stock, Mega Pixel, prapann, New Africa, Africa Studio, jamakosy, Pakhnyushchy. 6&7 - Quang Ho. 8&9 - Happy_Nati, photka. 10&11 - Dalibor Danilovic, Bannafarsai_Stock. 11 - Karin Hildebrand Lau/ Shutterstock. 12&13 - LightField Studios, Photographee.eu. 14 - Hue Ta/Shutterstock. 15 - Robie Online/Shutterstock. 14&15 - rangizzz, Elizabeth A.Cummings, sirtravelalot, wavebreakmedia, siam.pukkato, Air Images. 16&17 - Hunter Bliss Images, safakcakir. 18&19 - jamakosy, Jat306, Malachy666, design56, Volodymyr Krasyuk, bigacis, CK Bangkok Photography, Venus Kaewyoo, Marine's, AngieYeoh. 20&21 - wavebreakmedia, Kostikova Natalia, OnlyZoia. 22 - format35/iStock. 23 - Zerbor/Shutterstock. 22&23 - MarkoBr, Photographee.eu, LI CHAOSHU. Images are courtesy of Shutterstock.com. With thanks to Getty Images, Thinkstock Photo, and iStockphoto.

Library of Congress Cataloging-in-Publication Data

Names: Nelson, Louise, author.
Title: Life of a piece of paper / by Louise Nelson.
Description: Fusion books. | Minneapolis, Minnesota : Bearport Publishing Company, [2023] | Series: Eco journey | Includes index.
Identifiers: LCCN 2021061527 (print) | LCCN 2021061528 (ebook) | ISBN 9781636919003 (library binding) | ISBN 9781636919058 (paperback) | ISBN 9781636919102 (ebook)
Subjects: LCSH: Waste paper--Recycling--Juvenile literature. | Recycling (Waste, etc.)--Juvenile literature. | Recycled products--Juvenile literature.
Classification: LCC TS1120.5 .N4525 2022 (print) | LCC TS1120.5 (ebook) | DDC 676/.142--dc23/eng/20220118
LC record available at https://lccn.loc.gov/2021061527
LC ebook record available at https://lccn.loc.gov/2021061528

© 2023 Booklife Publishing
This edition is published by arrangement with Booklife Publishing.

North American adaptations © 2023 Bearport Publishing Company. All rights reserved. No part of this publication may be reproduced in whole or in part, stored in a retrieval system, or transmitted in any form or by any means, electronic, mechanical, photocopying, recording, or otherwise, without written permission from the publisher.

For more information, write to Bearport Publishing, 5357 Penn Avenue South, Minneapolis, MN 55419. Printed in the United States of America.

Contents

The Life of a Piece of Paper 4
What Is Paper? 6
Using Paper 8
Paper in Landfills 10
What Is Recycling? .12
Recycling Paper 14
Becoming New Paper . . . . 16
Trash to Treasure 18
Reuse and Upcycle 20
The Eco Journey of a Piece of Paper . . 22
Quick Quiz 23
Glossary 24
Index 24

The Life of a Piece of Paper

Paper is used for many things. You can draw on paper. The pages of books are paper. There's even toilet paper in the bathroom!

There are different types of paper. Paper can be thick or thin. It comes in different colors.

Do you know what happens to paper when you're done using it?

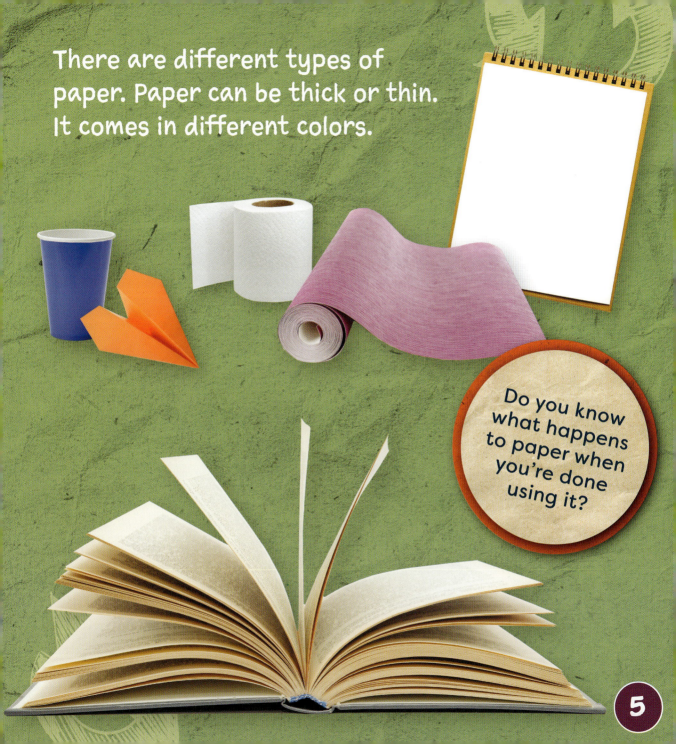

What Is Paper?

Pieces of paper are often smooth. They can be folded or ripped.

Paper is not heavy.

Paper is made from trees. Trees are cut down, and the wood is made into sticky, wet **pulp**. The pulp is dried in thin sheets that become paper.

Wood pulp

Billions of trees are cut down every year to make paper.

Using Paper

Paper items are usually made to be used only once. You can't use the same piece of paper over and over.

What paper items do you use?

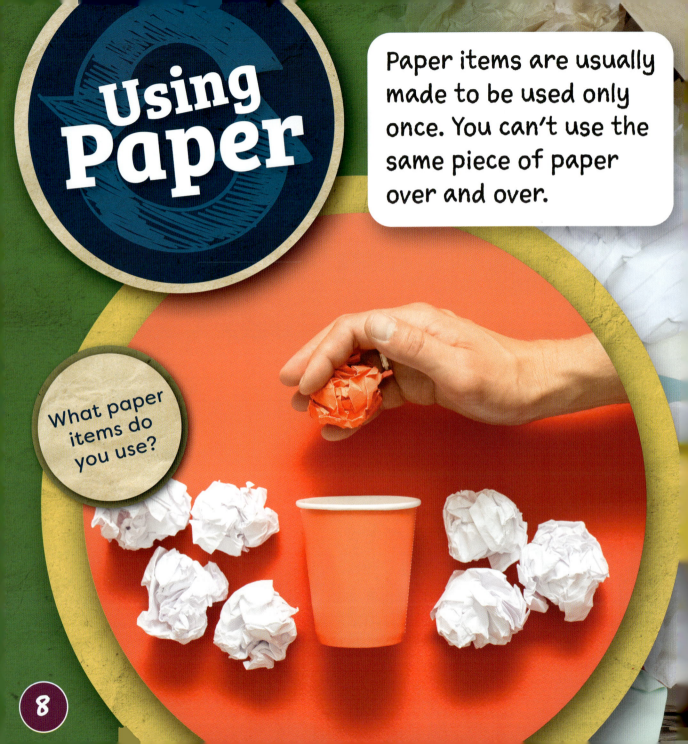

Paper cups and paper bags can't be used forever, either. What should you do with paper you can't use anymore?

Paper in Landfills

If you throw paper in the trash, it ends up in a **landfill**. Over time, paper breaks down and lets out a harmful **gas**. Too much of this gas is bad for Earth.

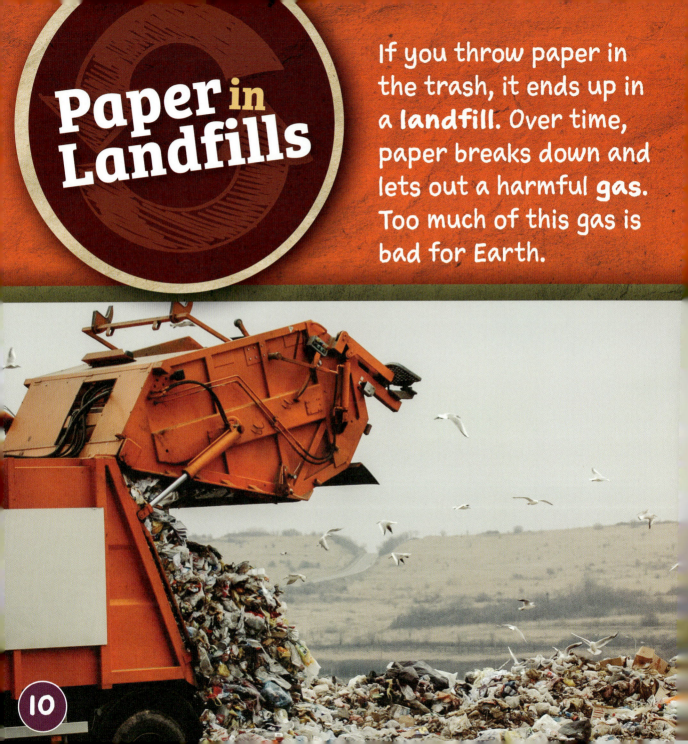

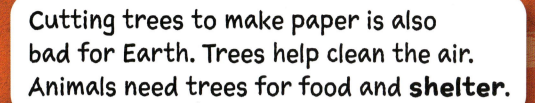

Cutting trees to make paper is also bad for Earth. Trees help clean the air. Animals need trees for food and **shelter**.

Trees take years to grow, but paper might be used for only a few seconds.

What Is Recycling?

Luckily, there's a way to keep paper out of landfills. We can **recycle** it!

Metal, plastic, and glass can be recycled, too.

Recycled paper is used to make new paper. This means we can cut down fewer trees.

A piece of paper can be recycled up to seven times.

Recycling Paper

Notebook paper, newspapers, and more can be put in recycling bins. But some paper can't be recycled. This may be different depending on where you live.

In most places, you can't recycle these items . . .

Receipts

Paper covered in foil or glitter

Paper with food stains

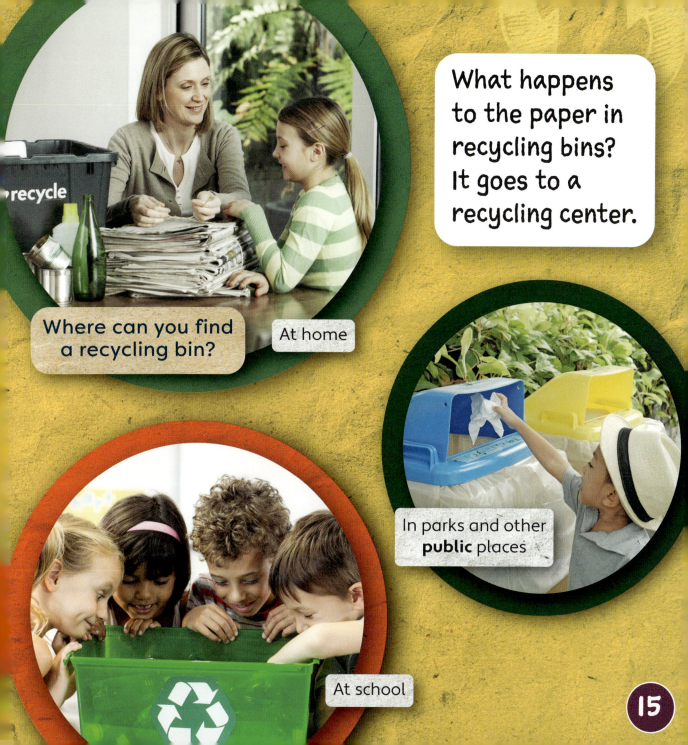

Becoming New Paper

At the recycling center, the paper is **sorted** into different types. Then, it is sent to a factory. The factory turns the paper into pulp.

Pulp

Before making pulp, factories wash paper to remove ink.

16

The pulp is dried in large, thin sheets. These are rolled up.

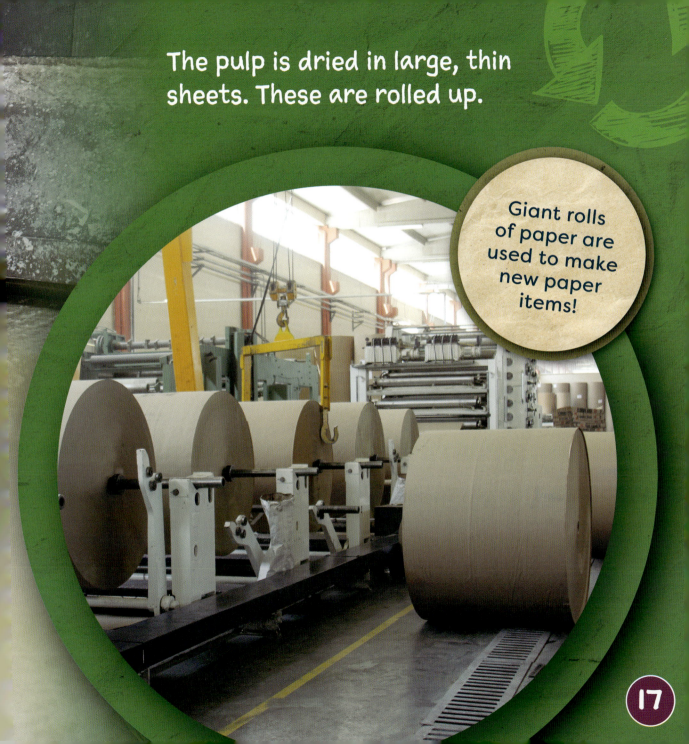

Giant rolls of paper are used to make new paper items!

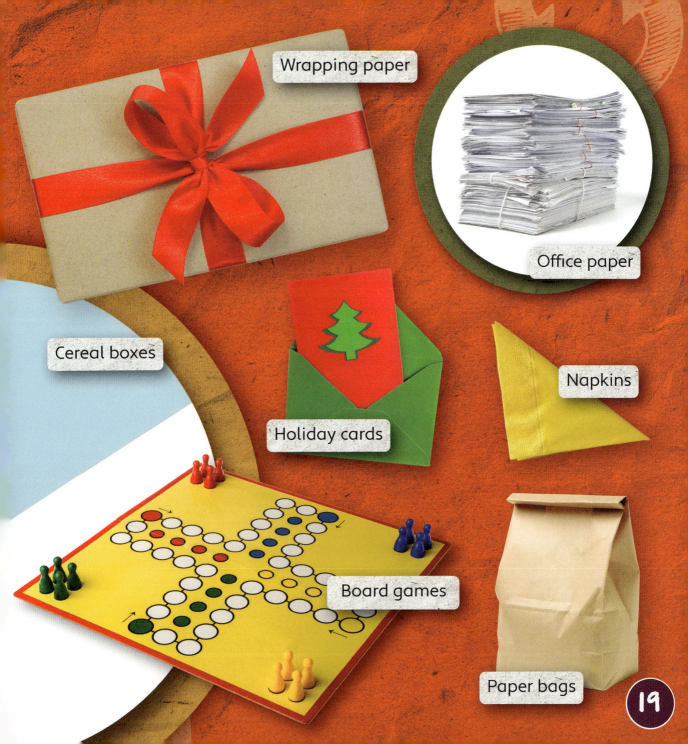

Reuse and Upcycle

Recycling helps Earth. But you can also help by reusing paper as much as possible! Write on both sides of paper. Try reusing wrapping paper.

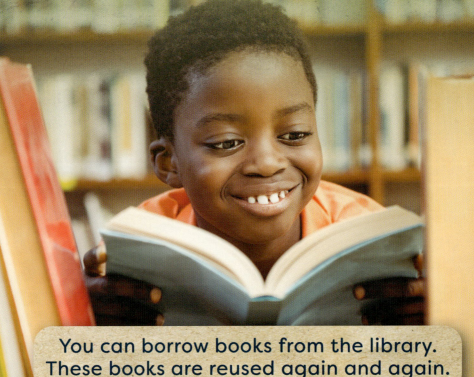

You can borrow books from the library. These books are reused again and again.

You can also reuse paper by upcycling it. Upcycling means making something old into something else. What could you make?

Crafts

Wrapping paper

The Eco Journey of a Piece of Paper

Paper is used.

The paper is put into a recycling bin to go to a recycling center.

The paper is sorted and made into pulp.

The pulp is dried into large rolls.

The recycled paper is made into something new.

Quick Quiz

Can you remember the eco journey of a piece of paper? Let's see! Look back through the book if you can't remember.

1. What is paper made from?
a) Trees
b) Flowers
c) Wheat

2. What is the wet stuff that recycled paper is made into before it becomes new paper?
a) Oatmeal
b) Pulp
c) Custard

3. How many times can paper be recycled?
a) Once, then it has to be thrown away
b) Up to seven times
c) 100 times

4. Which of these types of paper cannot be recycled?
a) Office paper
b) Newspaper
c) Receipts

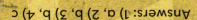
Answers: 1) a, 2) b, 3) b, 4) c

Glossary

gas a thing that is like air, which spreads out to fill any space available

landfill a large hole in the ground used for dumping garbage

public open to all people in the community

pulp a soft, wet mix

recycle to send something to be sorted and made into new materials

shelter a home or safe place to stay

sorted put into groups

Index

Earth 10–11, 20
factory 16
gas 10
landfill 10, 12
metal 12
pulp 7, 16–17, 22–23
recycling 12–16, 18, 20, 22–23
trees 7, 11, 13, 18, 23
upcycling 21